TABLE O

How I Fell In Love With Backyard Chickens

The Best Eggs You'll Ever Eat!

Getting Started

    Feeder

    Waterers

    Brooders

What Kind Of Chickens Should You Raise?

    Anconas

    Leghorn

    Silkies

    Rhode Island Reds

    Cornish

    Orpington

Eggs, Chicks, Or Pullets?

The Chicken Coop

Keeping Your Chickens Well-Fed

Breeding Chickens

Chicken Health Issues

    Lice

    Fleas

    Mites

    Worms

Eggs, Eggs, Eggs!

HOW I FELL IN LOVE WITH BACKYARD CHICKENS

My love affair with raising chickens in my backyard started off innocently enough. I was at a small farmers market in my neighborhood and ran into a guy selling free range eggs. The thing that really caught my attention though was just how much he was charging. He wanted $6 per dozen! I thought that was one of the craziest things I'd seen in awhile and continued shopping in other areas of the market. After all, I could easily buy a dozen eggs at the local super market for only $2 per dozen (or less).

After checking out the various things for sale at the farmers market, I made a full circle and found myself once again in front of the guy selling free range eggs. Something was different. In the span of only 20 minutes he had sold seven, maybe eight dozen eggs. To say I was surprised would be an understatement.

What was it that was so amazing about these eggs that people were actually willing to pay three times more for them than what the grocery store sold them for? I asked the guy selling them why this was so.

"Have you ever tried a fresh, free range egg?" He asked.

I hadn't.

He then proceeded to tell me just how much tastier they were than the store bought variety. Out of nothing more than a burning curiosity, I purchased a dozen of the eggs he was selling and took them home for a little culinary experimentation.

He was right.

These eggs were different – much tastier than any I'd ever had before. I definitely wanted more of these great eggs but wasn't willing to part with $6 every time I wanted to buy a dozen. That's when I stumbled upon a workable solution – I could raise my own chickens in my backyard and have a steady supply of these delicious eggs.

When I purchased my first three chicks, I didn't have anything like what you are reading now to guide me. I got information a little at a time from different sources – a few tips from the guy at the farm supply store, some information from an article in a magazine, and so forth until I was able to put all of the pieces of the puzzle together. This guide is the culmination of all my research (and trial and error). It's all you need to successfully raise your own backyard chickens so you can enjoy fresh and tasty eggs every day of the week.

THE BEST EGGS YOU'LL EVER EAT!

If you have never tried a fresh egg from a free range chicken (that is, an egg that was prepared the same day it was laid), you're really in for a surprise! Most people are really surprised to learn that fresh eggs are much tastier and even healthier than the eggs that are sold in grocery stores. They have darker, thicker yolks, and a noticeably improved taste that is impossible to describe (but amazingly good!). Studies have confirmed that fresh eggs have 1/3 less cholesterol, 25% less saturated fat, and more vitamins A, E, and omega 3's than eggs purchased from the store. In short, fresh eggs from your own chickens are super-eggs! Once you have tasted a truly fresh egg from a chicken you've raised yourself, you'll cringe at the thought of going back to eggs from the grocery store.

Why Raise Your Own Chickens?

Raising your own chickens is a great idea for many reasons. First of all, chickens make great pets! They are very gentle creatures and even ideal for small children. I'll bet you didn't even realize that chickens have their own personalities, too! It's true. Although you aren't going to be able to train your chickens to do neat tricks like you can with your dog and they won't want their ears scratched like your cat, chickens are still a lot of fun to have around the house. Chickens will eat out of your hand and will even come to you when called. Their individual personalities are unique and often amusing.

Perhaps one of the best things about fresh eggs from your own chickens is that you can literally have all that you want almost for free. You don't have to pay $6 a dozen at the local farmers market. You can raise your own chickens and collect your own fresh eggs on a daily basis. And it's probably a lot easier than you might have thought. These days more and more people are raising their own chickens in their backyards... and it's easy to see why. The free eggs are only one of the many benefits these little guys offer. Many people who live in cities are even raising their own chickens and cities all across the nation are changing their ordinances to be chicken-friendly (if you do live in a city or in town-limits, be sure to check your local ordinances before obtaining chickens).

Chickens also love to eat kitchen scraps. This is one of the great things about raising your own chickens. You don't have to spend a lot of money to feed them. They'll eat just about any leftover food items you've got. I've even seen my chickens eat leftover slices of pizza! Chickens also go totally crazy over bananas. You might be able to make an arrangement with your local grocery store to collect any over-ripe bananas they have for free instead of the store throwing them away. And when you let them out of their coop each morning, your chickens will be working all day long to rid your yard of insects. Because chickens eat copious amounts of insects and kitchen scraps, you'll only spend a few bucks each month on inexpensive store-bought chicken food.

Yet another benefit of raising your own chickens that you may not have thought of is that when you clean out your chickens' waste from their coop, you instantly have a free source of very high quality fertilizer for your vegetable or flower garden. Chicken droppings are a natural fertilizer that is very high in nitrogen and other nutrients. You can add chicken droppings directly to your garden or mix them in with your compost.

Chickens also make great pets because they require very little of your precious time. You'll only need to spend a couple of minutes each day to let them out of their coops in the morning, collect eggs, make sure they have enough food and water, and put them back up in the evenings. And here's a really neat fact about chickens... they put themselves up at night. When it gets dark chickens automatically know it's time to roost and make their way back to the coop themselves. There's no need to run around the yard gathering them up and herding them to the coop. They'll do that on their own. The only thing you need to do each evening is close the chicken coop door to protect them from predators. The only significant time you'll need to spend on taking care of your chickens is about one hour once a month to clean out the manure and dirty bedding material from their coop and replace it with fresh bedding. That's about it.

Taking Stock

The good news about raising your own chickens is that it takes very little to get started. You don't need to live on a farm either. All you need is a nice, big backyard. You will also need to obtain a chicken coop (which can be built very inexpensively), a feeder, a waterer, and a few other inexpensive items. Nearly all of the things you'll need can be purchased very inexpensively from your local farm supply store. And you certainly don't have to worry about the expense of baby chicks. Depending on the breed, you'll only spend between $2 – $3 per chick. We'll cover in detail everything you'll need to get started in the following chapters.

You only need three – maybe four chickens to get started, too. Hens are all you need – no roosters are necessary or even need apply. Hens can lay eggs without any roosters at all. How many eggs can you expect per hen? A good rule of thumb is to expect one egg per hen per day (although some breeds may lay less). So, if you have three hens, they could easily produce nearly two dozen eggs per week. Not bad at all!

One Small Caveat

There's one very important thing you should consider if you are thinking about raising your own chickens. Chickens require someone to let them out of their coops each morning and to put them up each night to protect them from predators (unless you have adequate fencing for your yard). And you'll need someone to collect eggs for you, too. If you have backyard chickens and you plan on being away for a day, the weekend, or are planning on taking a week long vacation, you'll need to arrange to have someone take care of these chores for you. Thankfully, this is usually very easy to do. All you have to do is offer a neighbor (or neighborhood kid) all the free eggs she can find while you're away and you will probably have people lining up to do the job for you.

GETTING STARTED

So you've decided that raising chickens is something you're definitely interested in. Good for you! You're really in for a treat. But at this point you're probably thinking, "Okay...What now? What's the first step I need to take to make this chicken thing happen?"

Space Requirements

The very first thing you'll want to consider – before you purchase your first chick – is how much space you have in your yard to raise chickens. If your available space is extremely limited, you may only be able to raise two or three hens, or none at all. On the other hand, there's always the chance that you may have more than sufficient space, enabling you to raise many hens and having enough eggs to give away to friends, neighbors, and family.

The good news about backyard chickens is that they require very little space to live and flourish. Remember, the hens that laid the eggs you buy in the grocery store were living in tiny cages with barely enough room to turn around. Chickens are hardy animals and don't require much space to be happy (okay, they do require more space than those tiny cages in the egg factories – but that's a given). As a general rule of thumb, the chickens you keep will need access to approximately four square feet of coop space and 10 square feet of outdoors space per chicken. As you can see, the space requirements to keep healthy (and happy) chickens are very low.

These space requirements aren't necessarily written in stone either, like some sort of chicken commandments that must never be broken. There is some degree of flexibility in them – especially when you consider the fact that some chicken breeds are bigger than others. Bantams, for example, are very small chickens and need less space than larger breeds. Jersey Giants, on the other hand, are quite large and will need additional space.

Another thing to consider before you leap into raising your own chickens is whether or not the space you intend for your chickens is already fenced in. This is a very important consideration. If your yard does not have existing fencing, you will need to have some installed. And even if your yard is already fenced in, you might want to partition a portion of your yard off just for your chickens. This means – extra fencing. Fencing materials can be expensive.

Hens Or Roosters – Or Both?

Another thing you'll want to consider prior starting your own personal chicken enterprise is your purpose for raising chickens. Do you want them only for the eggs? Are you interested in breeding chickens for their meat to be sure that the meat you and your family consumes is free from any antibiotics or potentially dangerous chemicals? These are important considerations and can be a determining factor over whether you end up with hens or hens and a rooster.

If you are primarily interested in raising chickens for the fresh eggs they produce, you do not need a rooster (a male chicken). Hens (female chickens) are all you need. These ladies will lay delicious eggs without a rooster being anywhere near them. Of course, the eggs will not be fertilized. This just means they don't have the ability to develop into little chicks, which leads us to...

If you are interested in breeding your chickens to enjoy the fun of raising new chicks each year or for their meat, you'll definitely need a rooster for your hens. The eggs simply cannot be fertilized without one. Unless you have a lot of chickens, you can probably get by with only one rooster. However, there's a very important thing you must consider before obtaining one. Roosters make noise – and lots of it. They make that lovely cockadoodle doo sound in the mornings, afternoons, evenings – essentially all day long. This can be a huge problem if you have neighbors living very close to you. Another thing to consider with roosters is they can be a little territorial and aggressive. If they suspect you are moving in on their territory (whatever that may be), they may try to attack you. Or they may not – roosters can definitely be odd. Hens, on the other hand, are usually very docile creatures and don't care one bit about you being around them.

If you do live in close proximity to neighbors, it might be a good idea to only purchase hens and to completely forget about roosters. They simply make too much noise to be worth the trouble. After all, you want your chickens to be able to live in harmony with their surroundings. That might be hard to do if you have neighbors secretly plotting their destruction to rid the neighborhood of noise pollution. Quiet hens equals happy neighbors.

Accessories

Aside from either building or buying a chicken coop (which we'll cover in a later chapter), you'll need to obtain a few inexpensive accessories to make sure your chickens are able to get plenty to eat and drink. Thankfully, these are very inexpensive and can be purchased at most farm supply stores or you can even construct your own from plans.

FEEDER

A feeder is a simple device that holds food for your chickens. If you do purchase commercial chicken feed, it's best to feed it to them in a feeder. If you just spread it around on the ground, there will be some wasted feed since the chickens will eat some and leave some. By using a feeder, you can minimize waste since the food is stored in one area for the chickens to come back to throughout the day. You can expect to pay anywhere from $10 to $30 for a good quality feeder, depending the complexity of construction.

WATERERS

All of your chickens should have access to clean, fresh water at all times. This isn't optional. To make sure your chickens have plenty of water, you'll need a waterer of some sort. You can either purchase a commercial-made waterer ($10 – $30) or you can even make one. A very simple and easy homemade waterer can be made by taking a gallon fruit or juice can and drilling a small 3/4" hole on the side of the can near the bottom. You then fill it with water and turn it upside down so that it sits in a pie pan. As long as you don't drill the hole higher than the edges of the pie pan, the pan will always be full of water (as long as you keep the can full, that is).

BROODERS

If you are starting your flock with young chicks, you will need some way to keep them warm until they grow big enough to fend for themselves. A brooder is any type of heat source combined with a simple box of some sort to keep your young chicks in and to keep them nice and warm. Most brooder heat sources are simple electric heat lamps and can be purchased for as little as $10 each. As far as the box goes, there are many different possibilities. There's no need to spend a lot of money on this since your chicks will only be using it for about four to six weeks. Some people use small cages while others use a large cardboard box. You could even put your chicks in an old unused aquarium. Most people make their own brooders. There's really no need to spend a lot of money on some kind of commercial model, especially when you are only going to be using it for such a short period of time.

When shopping for a heat source for your brooder, be sure to get one with a heat lamp of at least 250 watts. If you try to use a 60 or 100 watt bulb that was designed for a lamp in your living room, it's probably not going to deliver enough heat to do the job. Also, it's often a good idea to purchase a red lamp instead of a white light. The red light is not as harsh and makes it easier for them to sleep. The red light also tends to calm chicks and will actually prevent them from pecking on each other.

WHAT KIND OF CHICKENS SHOULD YOU RAISE?

One of the most important decisions you'll make in raising your own chickens is deciding which breed of chickens to go with. It's not always an easy decision to make. This is especially true when you consider the fact that there are so many different breeds to choose from. In addition to the nearly countless pure breeds that exist, there are also many hybrids you can purchase, too. In short, there are literally hundreds of potential breeds to choose from. Let's narrow it down to a few great choices.

If you are new to raising chickens, there are a few characteristics you'll want in the chickens you raise. First, you'll want your chickens to be friendly and easy to get along with. Who wants chickens with attitude problems? Second, you definitely want your chickens to be easy to take care of. High maintenance chickens need not apply. Third, you want to obtain chickens that grow fast and lay a lot of eggs. And finally, you'll want to obtain chickens that are very common so you can easily find them at your local farm supply store or even through a mail order catalog.

Chickens For Meat Or Chickens For Eggs

One thing you'll definitely need to consider before you purchase your first chicken is whether you intend to raise your chickens for their meat, for their eggs, or both. It does matter because some breeds of chickens are better egg layers than others while some are better suited for their meat.

BANTAMS

If the space you have allocated for raising your chickens is truly limited, you may be able to get by with bantams. Bantams are a very small type of chicken that many keep for pets or to show in exhibits. They do produce eggs but they are very small. To get the equivalent of one regular chicken egg, you will need three bantam eggs. Still, these little guys could be just the answer if your space is limited and you still desire free range eggs. If you are considering bantams, it's important to keep in mind that there are many different kinds of bantam breeds to consider. Bantam simply refers to a particular variety of chicken...not a particular breed.

ANCONAS

Anconas are often considered to be a good breed for beginners. These beautiful black and white chickens lay white eggs and are very easy to take care of. The only real negative to this bread is that it does have a tendency to try to fly around a bit.

LEGHORN

The leghorn is another breed that is a good choice for beginners. Leghorns are usually white but may also be brown, red, silver, or black. These hens lay large, white eggs and many commercial egg companies use this breed because of the many eggs they lay. An adult hen can lay more than 300 eggs per year.

SILKIES

Silkies are often considered to be very attractive hens with feathers that have a rather fluffy plumage. Silkies are often seen in poultry competitions but...guess what? They are also great chickens for beginners to raise. They are very docile chickens, make great pets, and you can expect an output of somewhere in the neighborhood of three to five eggs each week per hen.

RHODE ISLAND REDS

The Rhode Island Red gets its name at least partly from its red feathers. The breed is very hardy and easy to take care of. You can expect a yield of around 300 eggs per year per hen.

CORNISH

The cornish breed of chicken is not particularly well-suited for egg production. Nevertheless, it is a very popular choice for those who are interested in raising their own chickens for the meat. Males can reach a weight of up to 11 pounds while hens usually top out at eight pounds, which is a good amount of meat per chicken.

Plymouth Rocks – This breed of chicken should be considered for those who are interested in raising chickens for both their eggs and their meat. As such, Plymouth Rocks are considered dual-purpose chickens. They can grow to a weight of 7.5 to 10 lbs and you can expect an approximate egg production of around 200 brown eggs per hen annually.

ORPINGTON

If I had to pick out the one single best breed of chicken for beginners, it would be the Orpington, hands down. What's so special about this bread? A lot. For one thing, Orpingtons are very docile chickens and are great around kids. These little guys love to have contact with humans and will even do little things to try to get your attention. Orpingtons have great personalities and are a lot of fun to keep around. Believe it or not, you can even get an Orpington chicken to sit in your lap! Orpingtons are also prolific egg layers and some hens can lay up to one egg per day.

Where Do You Get Your Chickens From?

There are many different places you can obtain chickens from including your local farmers market, a local farm supply store, someone in your neighborhood who raises chickens, and even mail order. Yes, mail order! As you can see, obtaining chickens is not difficult at all.

The mail order option is very interesting. There are many people who order live chickens and have them sent through the mail all the time. I had an interesting conversation with a rural mail carrier one day and he told me you can occasionally hear chickens clucking from somewhere in the stack of boxes they are getting ready to deliver. I'm not going to make any recommendations on any particular company if you are considering ordering online. You can easily find many great companies to choose from though by simply doing an internet search for "mail order chickens" or "order chickens through the mail."

EGGS, CHICKS, OR PULLETS?

Okay, now that we've established that there are many different places you can get your chickens from, should you purchase grown chickens, baby chicks, or fertilized eggs? In other words, which should come first...the chicken or the egg? (sorry...couldn't resist)

Eggs

If you purchase fertilized eggs to hatch yourself, you'll have to come up with some way to incubate them yourself since you won't have a hen to sit on them and keep them warm. Purchasing an incubator is an extra expense but the sheer joy of hatching your own eggs is almost irresistible for many people. Kids love to watch chicks hatch from eggs, too. What a great educational experience! If you have kids, you should definitely consider starting your own flock by hatching your own eggs. The extra expense of purchasing an incubator is totally worth it.

There are a couple of negative aspects of hatching your chickens from eggs that you should be aware of. First, you have to wait for them to grow up and mature before they can start laying eggs. This means you'll have a waiting period of about six months after they hatch before you can expect any eggs for your omelets. Second, you might not get all hens in your eggs. If you decide that you have enough space to raise five hens and you purchase five fertilized eggs, you could easily end up with one or two roosters in the bunch. And you have to wait several months for them to mature before you identify the hens from the roosters. If you are not able to raise roosters because of the noise they make, you'll have to find a way to get rid of them after all you've gone through to hatch them and raise them.

Chicks

If raising chickens from eggs sounds like it's more complicated than it's worth, the next thing to consider is raising young chicks. Chicks are very inexpensive and can often be purchased for usually no more than $3 each. If you do decide to raise chicks, however, you will need to purchase a brooder (which we previously discussed) to make sure your chicks stay nice and warm for their first few weeks of life. By the way, you'll also need a brooder if you raise your chickens from eggs, too. You don't need to keep them in a brooder for very long though. After about four weeks you can transition them to a coop. You'll be surprised at how fast your chicks grow!

Raising your chicks in a brooder is a fairly simple affair. First, it's important to make sure the floor of your brooder is lined with some sort of soft material. There are many suitable materials you can use such as straw, sawdust, fine mulch, or even shredded paper. There's no need to spend a lot of money on the flooring since you'll need to change it periodically to keep your chicks clean from their own waste. And naturally, you'll need to keep an adequate supply of food and water for your little guys, too.

You'll need to purchase chick starter feed but thankfully it is very inexpensive. You can purchase a five pound bag for between $7 - $8. Whatever type of box you decide to raise your chicks in, be sure it's at least 12 inches high to make sure they can't easily escape. And do get a container that's big enough for your chicks to move around in. You'll want at least .5 square foot of space per chick at a minimum.

One square foot of space per chick is preferable. You'll also want to cover your box with something to keep them from escaping, being mindful that they need plenty of ventilation to let fresh air in. A wire mesh screen works well for this purpose. Suitable containers include such things as a glass or acrylic fish tank, a cardboard or wooden box, a large plastic storage bin, or other similar containers.

Be very, very careful when attaching your heat lamp to the box you'll be keeping your chicks in. Be absolutely certain that the heat source is far enough away from the box so that there is no risk of starting a fire. It's usually best to suspend the heat source so that it is over the middle of the box. You want to make sure the heat is evenly distributed so that there are no hot or cold spots.

Temperature control is a pretty big deal when raising chicks. If your little guys get too cold, they may die. If they get too hot, that can also cause them to die. There's a generally accepted protocol you should follow when raising your chicks under the light of a brooder. Each week you will want to lower the temperate a certain amount as follows:

Age Of Chick	Temperature In Fahrenheit
1 week	90 – 95 degrees
2 weeks	85 – 90 degrees
3 weeks	80 – 85 degrees
4 weeks	75 – 80 degrees
5 weeks	70 – 75 degrees

You can usually do away with the heat lamp once you get the temperature down to 70 degrees if you are doing this indoors since this is usually room temperature anyway. Also, if you have several chicks in one box, you can usually go with the lower temperate in the above temperature ranges since groups of chicks keep each other warm. If you have just a few chicks, go with the higher temperature.

Also, the above temperatures are not absolute rules that must be followed either. It's important to pay very close attention to the behavior of your chicks. For example, if you see a group of them huddled together, this may indicate that they are too cool and the temperature may need to be turned up.

On the other hand, if you observe your chicks continually staying apart from each other or hanging out in the corners of the box, you may have the temperature too high and need to lower it. Chicks that are too hot may also appear to be panting (breathing heavily with their beaks open). This is another clue that you may have things a little too hot for them.

Your chicks' mannerisms are very important and offer a lot of insight into how they are doing. For the most part your chicks should be making happy little "peep" noises when they are awake in addition to walking around, drinking water, and pecking at their food. And of course, they should be able to go to sleep when they are tired. This stuff isn't rocket science.

There's one last thing to consider if you are raising chicks. Like hatching eggs, there's always the chance that some of your little guys could turn out to be roosters. While there are methods of determining a young chick's sex, it's not a simple process. Commercial poultry farms do it all the time but for the backyard chicken enthusiast, your best bet on determine whether you have little hens or little roosters is to simply let them grow up and see how they turn out. And of course, if you do end up with a few roosters, you may have to get rid of them to keep the neighbors happy.

Pullets

If you want to be absolutely certain you are getting a backyard full of hens and don't want to risk ending up with a few roosters and having to start all over, the best way to go is with pullets. A pullet is a young hen that is almost ready to start laying eggs (usually about 17 weeks old). Generally, hens start laying eggs when they are about 5 – 6 months old, so you will still have a just few more weeks of waiting for fresh eggs for your omelets if you go with pullets.

Naturally, pullets cost more than chicks since they have already received several months of care and feeding. That doesn't mean they are prohibitively expensive though. You can purchase pullets via mail order for $10 – $15 each, depending on breed. In addition, definitely check your local classifieds (such as Craigslist) for pullets, too, especially if you live in an area with a lot of farmers nearby. You can get some great deals by going with a local supplier.

Aside from not having to worry about ending up with any roosters, pullets are also a good choice for the novice chicken enthusiast because you can completely skip the aggravation and expense associated with the construction of a brooder. Your new hens are ready to be introduced to their coop and outdoor environment the first day you get them.

"Retiring" Your Aging Hens

Although chickens live 8 – 10 years on average (some can even live up to 20 years!), not all of those years are prime egg producing years. Hens don't suddenly stop laying eggs. Rather, they slowly decrease the number of eggs they lay as they get older. If you are keeping your hens primarily for the eggs they produce, at some point you are going to have to retire your girls as they age and replace them with younger hens.

It does make sense to do so since your older hens eat just as much chicken feed as the younger hens do without producing as many eggs. So, unless your older hens have become irreplaceable family pets, it's a good idea to periodically "retire" them.

So, when exactly should you retire your hens? How old should they be when it's time for them to call it quits? There's no hard and fast rule for this. You can play it by ear on this one and retire each individual hen when the amount of eggs she produces has noticeably declined. Some will let their hens go at two years, others at three years, and some may even hold out until five or more years of age. It's a decision you'll have to make separately for each individual hen.

So, what exactly does it mean to "retire" a hen? Is there a special retirement community for old hens? Unfortunately, there's no special place for aging hens where they live peaceful lives crocheting, golfing, and perpetually complaining about the weather. When we say "retire," we are referring to getting rid of them. And this means either giving them away or slaughtering them for their meat.

Slaughtering your own chickens for meat in your backyard may be somewhat problematic if you live in a close-knit community. Your neighbors may not care too much for the sight of seeing a chicken slaughtered. Even though tens of thousands of chickens are slaughtered on a daily basis in commercial chicken farms to provide all of the chicken nuggets, chicken breasts, and countless other chicken meat variations we find in our grocery stores and in fast-food and other restaurants, many people do find the process of slaughtering a chicken hard to watch. For this one reason alone, you might want to skip slaughtering your own chickens and just give them away instead.

Who will take an aging hen that isn't in prime egg producing shape anymore? You would be surprised. Many people will want the fresh chicken for its meat and will take care of the slaughtering process on their own, away from your home. If you have one or more fresh hens to give away, you can easily put an advertisement in Craigslist to give them away.

After giving away your aging hens, the fastest way to enjoy fresh eggs again is to purchase pullets and integrate them in with your existing flock.

THE CHICKEN COOP

One of the most important considerations in raising your own chickens is their housing. A house for chickens is most commonly called a chicken "coop." Coops are available in many different styles and designs and the type you go with should be based on a careful consideration of the amount of available space you have and the number of birds and breed you are raising.

Buy or Build?

One very important thing you'll want to consider is whether you should purchase a chicken coop or build one. In my own personal shopping experiences, I've discovered that pre-built chicken coops are almost always very, very expensive. It generally doesn't matter whether you are purchasing a local handmade coop or a plastic model from a mail order company, they all tend to come with a very high price tag. I was shopping in a farmer's market one day, for example, and encountered a very small coop that was only suited for two to three small hens, at best. Curious, I looked at the price tag and was very surprised to see a list price of $300! Unless your construction skills are nearly non-existent, I always recommend building a chicken coop instead of buying one. You can literally save hundreds of dollars by building your own. And not only that but a coop can be made with inexpensive (or free) scrap materials from another construction project. It's also very easy to find low-cost or free plans for chicken coops, too. A simple internet search for "free chicken coop plans" or "chicken coop plans" usually turns up many great options.

As a side note, if you are someone who enjoys building things, you could easily start a small side business building chicken coops and selling them through local classified listings or through Craigslist.

Space Requirements

The size of your chicken coop depends a lot on how much free outdoors space your birds have to frolic and run around in. If they have a lot of outdoors space, it is unlikely that they will spend much time in their coop...mainly during rainy days and when they are sleeping or laying eggs. As such, they will not need a very large coop. However, if you have very little available outdoors space, you will need much bigger housing to make sure they have adequate space for exercise, roosting, egg laying, and all of their other activities. For those with very small backyards, a coop of 5 x 7 ft. is adequate for six to 12 hens. Smaller coops are fine for those with larger backyards.

Another thing to consider is that there will be times when you will need a separate coop to take care of a sick hen or a hen who is taking care of her chicks. Thankfully, very little space is required for these purposes and you can often get away with using a large pet travel carrier for these temporary coop needs.

Different Types of Coops

Chicken coops can be broken down into two different types...the portable coop (which is occasionally referred to as a chicken tractor) and permanent housing.

The chicken tractor may be the best option for raising backyard chickens. A chicken tractor is a small coop (or sometimes a large coop) that has wheels on it to make moving it from one location to another very easy.

Some chicken tractor designs have handles on one end like a wheelbarrow design which makes moving the coop very easy.

Why would you want a mobile chicken coop? It's simple, really. From time to time you'll need to move your coop to fresh ground if or when the ground beneath it becomes a muddy mess. Since most coops sit directly on the ground with the chickens having access to the ground beneath, it doesn't take long before they completely scratch up all of the grass.

During rainy seasons, water mixes with the bare ground and quickly makes mud. Having the ability to quickly move your coop to a place with fresh grass means you don't have to let the ground get in bad shape to start with. You can simply relocate the coop once every couple of weeks (or however often you desire).

There are some who prefer a more permanent structure for their chickens. Permanent housing is usually much more sturdy than chicken tractors and may make sense for you if you have an outbuilding of some kind that you can convert into a coop. If you do decide to convert an existing structure, be sure you are able to provide your birds with adequate ventilation in the form of windows with mesh wiring over them.

If a coop does not have adequate air circulation, the air inside the coop could become too warm for your hens to comfortably lay on their eggs. In addition, Stale air in the coop during both the warmer and cooler months could contribute to the spread of disease. And of course, you want to make sure that any gases that are created from your birds' droppings are adequately vented to prevent any sickness from that.

Nest Boxes

Regardless of whether you decide to go with a chicken tractor or more permanent housing, the coop you buy or build should have some simple nest boxes for your hens. You'll need at least one nest box for every three egg laying hens you have. The nest box does not have to be anything fancy. A simple wooden box will do just fine. The box should be 12 inches square and about 14 inches high. Place the nest box in a relatively dark part of the coop, since this is the type of environment chickens like to lay eggs in.

The nest boxes you create for your hens will also need some sort of bedding material for them to lay eggs in. A variety of inexpensive (or free) bedding materials can be used including wood shavings, shredded newspaper, straw, and even leaves. Regardless of which type of bedding you decide to go with, be sure it's not damp or moldy to prevent the spread of disease. When placing the bedding material in each nest box, be sure it's at least five to six inches deep.

Perches

When chickens sleep at night, they prefer to do so from some sort of perch. A perch is simply long piece of wood that is elevated off the ground that chickens like to hang onto while they sleep. The thickness of the boards you use for normal size birds (not bantams) should be at least three inches wide and two inches thick. And of course, the top part (the part the birds grasp onto) must have a rounded edge. You should allocate at least eight inches of perch space per bird.

Positioning the Coop

Where you place your chicken coop is far more important than you might think. Chickens hate to get their feet wet so you want to make sure you place it in an area that is well-drained. It's also important to realize that chickens do not possess sweat glands and although they do like warm temperatures, they do not like conditions of extreme heat. The perfect location for your coop will have some kind of wind break as well as adequate shelter from both the sun and rain.

Cleaning the Coop

In a perfect world all chickens would only relieve themselves outside of their coop. But guess what? We don't live in a perfect world and chickens do, indeed, "go" in their coop. Because of this, you'll need to clean the coop out on a regular basis. It's a good idea to develop a regular routine to make sure the coop does not end up with too much build up. Thankfully though, it's not as big a chore as you might think. You should plan on taking a few minutes at least once a week to clean out the droppings from the coop.

You will also need to periodically clean out the nest boxes but not nearly as often as the rest of the coop. For the nest boxes you can usually get by with cleaning them out once per month in the summertime and once every two months during the winter. When you do clean out the nest boxes you should completely replace the bedding material.

KEEPING YOUR CHICKENS WELL-FED

What is the one thing that makes the eggs from backyard chickens taste so much better than store-bought eggs? The number one factor that influences this is their diet. Chickens that are raised in egg factories are fed a diet of corn, some vitamin supplements, and little else. Backyard chickens, on the other hand, enjoy a very diverse diet consisting of seeds, herbs, grubs, insects, in addition to any commercial feed you add to their diets.

In a wild setting, chickens can obtain all the nutrition they need from their near-constant foraging. However, in a domesticated setting, it's a good idea to supplement your chicken's diet with some kind of commercial chicken feed to make sure they get all of the carbohydrates, fats, and other vitamins and minerals they need to be happy and healthy.

Water

It almost goes without saying but it's definitely worth repeating. Never let your chickens go without a good supply of clean, fresh water. If you are unsure of how much they will need or if you plan on being away for a period of time, you can always purchase an inexpensive kiddie pool and fill it up for your chickens to drink from.

When to Feed Your Chickens

The best time to feed your chickens is first thing in the morning after they come down from their roosts after a good night's rest. If you are using any commercial feed, it's best to give them this feed in the morning. Your chickens will then forage for grubs and other insects the rest of the day. If you have any table scraps, you can give them to your chickens as the scraps become available.

Storing Chicken Food

Be sure to keep any commercial chicken food you purchase in a cool, dry place and away from any other animals that might be tempted to nibble on it. For maximum protection you can keep the food in large, plastic containers with tight sealing lids.

Table Scraps

We've already briefly mentioned the fact that adult chickens love to eat table scraps. This is one way you can provide additional (and free) food to your chickens to serve the dual-purpose of enhancing their diet in addition to getting rid of your unwanted leftovers. Chickens love table scraps and will gladly eat any leftover fruits, cheese, pasta, cereal, vegetables, and even breads that you have.

Food for Chicks

If you are starting out with baby chicks, you will need to purchase special "starter" feed just for them. Don't even attempt to feed your newborns with adult feed or table scraps. Adult chicken feed is specially formulated to give hens all the nutrients they need to produce high-quality eggs. And table scraps may be difficult for your little guys to eat and digest. Starter feed, on the other hand, is carefully formulated with just the right amount of protein they will need to ensure they are properly nourished. You can usually discontinue starter feed when your chicks are at least four weeks old and let them start to eat adult feed.

Some starter feeds are medicated while others are not. Medicated starter feeds contain a special medication in them to prevent chicks from contracting coccidia, which is an infection that kills many chicks. Whether your decide to go with a medicated starter feed or not is purely a judgment call. Some prefer to protect their chicks from this disease while others believe the chicks need to be able to develop an immunity to it on their own. Incidentally, coccidia is usually picked up from chicken droppings. You can do a lot to prevent any onset of this disease by keeping your brooder clean.

Mash or Pellets?

When you purchase commercial chicken feed, you have two main options: mash or pellets. Mash is a mix of a variety of grain-based ingredients that have been ground into a fine mix. A pellet, on the other hand, is mash that has been compressed into a small mass. Both pellets and mash have their own advantages and disadvantages. Pellets are very easy for chickens to eat and chickens usually waste much less of their food this way. However, pellets may be too big for younger chickens to handle. Also, when you feed your chickens pellets, they tend to quickly fill up on them and tend to be bored until their stomachs empty and they are hungry again. The main benefit of mash is that it is very easy for chickens of nearly all ages to eat and you can even mix in some table scraps with your mash. Chickens also don't fill up their stomachs as quickly on mash as they will with pellets. They may eat a little bit of mash and then proceed to hunt around the yard for grubs and other insects. The downside with mash, as previously mentioned, is that chickens do tend to spread it around as they eat, resulting in some degree of waste. Mash can also be messy for chickens to eat and they can easily end up with it encrusted on their feathers and beaks.

True Grit

Chickens have a special digestion requirement that you should definitely be aware of. To help them properly digest the food they eat, chickens consume small stones (called grit) on a regular basis. Small stones found on the ground usually don't work too well since they are rounded. Because of this you'll need to purchase grit from a farm supply store for your birds. One bag of grit will probably last a long time since each bird will only consume approximately one ounce of grit per month. Keep the grit separate from your chicken's food. Do not mix the two together. It's always best to keep the grit in a separate container.

Commercial Supplements – Vitamins and Minerals

If you walk down the chicken isle of your local farm supply store, you are sure to encounter a variety of vitamin and mineral supplements that you can purchase. Although the temptation to purchase these supplements may be strong, you can take a pass on them. If you are feeding your chickens commercial chicken feed, they are probably getting all of the vitamins and minerals they need. In fact, some commercial chicken feed even comes fortified with extra supplements to make sure your birds get plenty of nutrition.

BREEDING CHICKENS

At some point in your backyard chicken adventure you may get to the point where you want to get into breeding chickens, either for the fun of watching new chicks develop and hatch from eggs or even as a way to replace older hens. Regardless of your reasons, breeding chickens is truly fascinating and satisfying. Children and adults alike are always fascinated as new life pecks its way out of its shell and starts flitting around.

If you are interested in breeding your hens but you don't currently have a rooster due to neighbor issues, you're going to have to get one (or get temporary access to one) or else it's game over for breeding. It is possible to borrow a rooster for a short period (perhaps a month, or so) and then return it to its owner.

You can ask around at your local farm supply store to see if they know anyone who would be willing to do this or even ask around at your local farmers market. And you might be able to get away with some temporary crowing from a rooster as long as you let your neighbors know in advance that it's only a temporary arrangement. And of course, you can always coax them into the idea by offering them some fresh eggs from your flock.

Is Your Hen Broody?

If your plans are to have one or more of your hens lay on fertilized eggs and hatch them the natural way, you will need to make sure your hens are broody. A broody hen is one that is ready to sit on eggs for long periods of time. You can tell if your hens are ready (broody) simply by observing them. A hen that is broody will sit in her nest box much longer than is the norm, often for several days at a time. You can test her by placing a hand underneath her to see how she reacts. If she tries to peck at your hand or generally disapproves of what you are doing, she is probably broody and is in the mood to lay on some eggs.

Hens Vs. Incubators

Is hatching eggs with hens always the best way to go? What about using incubators? While it may at first seem like incubators pose an easy solution to a hen that isn't broody, trying to hatch eggs this way isn't always easy. Nevertheless, an incubator may be necessary since you can't always count on having a broody hen available when you need it.

There are two basic types of incubators you can purchase to hatch eggs in. And thankfully, the one you'll probably end up getting is not expensive. The first incubator type is the cabinet type and the second is a type that uses still air to do the job. The cabinet type is probably more complex than what you'll need for your backyard chickens since they usually have several levels of trays for eggs. For the most part these incubators are designed for commercial chick hatcheries. A simple (yet effective) still air model is probably all you'll ever need.

When incubating eggs, be sure to be vigilant on the humidity level in the incubator. This is one of the most important things to be aware of because eggs can lose water (and density) through evaporation. Be sure to carefully follow the instructions that come with the particular incubator model you purchase to be sure you keep the humidity level at an optimal level.

Check Your Eggs With Candling

If you are using an incubator to hatch eggs, it's a good idea to check the status of the eggs at least once per week to make sure they are developing properly. The easiest method to do this is with candling. Candling is simply a process whereby you hold an egg (in a darkened environment) in front of a bright light to see the contents. It's kind of like x-ray for eggs (without the dangerous radiation). You can purchase an inexpensive commercial candler for this purpose or you can even make your own out of a cardboard tube lined with tin foil. You can cut an egg-shaped hole to view the egg in the middle of the tube. Simply shine a strong flashlight in one of the tube and you should have a good view of egg development.

Okay, now that we've established that candling is a good thing to do, what exactly should you look for while you're using your new powers of x-ray to check them out. The purpose of candling is to make sure everything is progressing as it should be inside the egg. You can easily tell if an egg has been fertilized in the first five to seven days. Under the candle you should be able to see blood vessels in the embryo as well as an air sac. If at the two week period you don't see any blood vessels or air sac, you should remove it from the incubator (or hen) to prevent any type of contamination.

Hatching Chicks

If you are using a broody hen to hatch your eggs, you will want to transfer both hen and chicks to a separate (and temporary) coop after all hatching has been completed. You can either build a separate coop for this purpose or you can use a travel pet carrier for a large dog. If you do use a pet travel carrier, be sure you get one that is large enough for them to have room to move around in. Also, it's important not to confine your hen and chicks to their temporary coop. You want them to have access to their own space with short grass so they can move around some. After your chicks have hatched you can feed them commercial chick feed for the first four weeks. Also, be sure they have plenty of water to drink in a container that is not too deep to make sure they don't fall in and drown. Don't be too concerned if your chicks don't eat anything for the first 24 hours after they've hatched since they still have some nutritional reserves from their yolks still in their systems.

If you have hatched your eggs in an incubator, you will need to keep them in a brooder for the next few weeks to simulate the warmth and conditions of maturing under the wings of a broody hen. We've already discussed brooder operations in a previous chapter so we won't get back into it here (no need for repetition).

After a period of several weeks in the brooder, your chicks will have gained substantial size. They can then be taken outside and placed in a small, closed-off area of grass where they can be introduced to the outdoors life. It almost goes without saying that when you do introduce your chicks to the great outdoors, be sure you place them in an area where cats and other predators who might think little chicks are quite tasty don't have access to them.

CHICKEN HEALTH ISSUES

Chickens are very hardy animals and for the most part, they do extremely well in many different climates and environments. As long as you keep your chickens' coop clean, provide them with a good amount of yard space to run around in, and make sure they have a healthy diet with plenty of fresh water, your chickens should thrive and provide you with a steady production of eggs. However, as with all things in life, there's no guarantee that your birds will never encounter any health issues. Because of this, it's important for us to take a good look at a few health issues you should be aware of.

How Do You Know When A Chicken Is Sick?

Perhaps the first step in taking care of a sick chicken is being able to identify that you do, indeed, have a sick bird. It's not as hard as may think to make this determination. There are a few specific signs you can look for that will clue you in.

You can tell a lot about the health of your chickens just by watching them. Chickens tend to stay close to the flock so if you see one that stays off to itself for an extended period of time, that might be an indication that something is wrong. You should also be on the lookout for normal chicken behavior. Chickens spend the better part of their days hanging out with the flock and scratching and pecking around for food. Any deviation from this normal behavior should be cause for concern. And finally, you can periodically do a physical inspection of your birds to look for any signs of disease such as a dramatic weight loss, patches of missing feathers, as well as insect problems such as mites, lice, fleas, and other unwelcome creatures living in your chickens' feathers.

Although rare, if you do suspect you have a sick bird on your hands that has a virus of some kind, you should consult with a veterinarian for the appropriate treatment. Nevertheless, there are a few simple things you can take care of yourself. Let's check them out...

Dealing With Parasites

Like most farm animals, chickens do occasionally end up with some kind of parasite issues. A few possibilities include lice, worms, mites, and fleas. Treating these conditions is very simple.

LICE

Lice is usually easily visible by doing a quick examination by parting the feathers. If lice is present, you can often see them moving around on the skin. Lice eggs look like tiny yellow or white dots. They closely resemble dandruff on humans. If you do detect lice on any of your birds, you can take care of it by dusting each bird with a simple louse powder.

FLEAS

Fleas are usually easily spotted without having to do any special inspection. If you do detect fleas, you can treat each individual bird with a simple flea powder.

MITES

Spotting mites on chickens can be a bit tricky since these little creatures burrow beneath the skin. You can often tell if your birds have mites by looking for swollen and crusty skin, whether on their legs or around the facial area. You can treat an area that is infested with mites by coating it in petroleum jelly. This prevents the mites from getting the air they need to live and ensures a quick eradication.

WORMS

Tapeworms and roundworms are the two most common types of worm infestations that chickens have to deal with. Both types of worms are passed through fecal matter. The most common way chickens become infected with these parasites is when they eat insects that have eaten fecal matter with worm eggs in it. Birds with tapeworms may have trouble gaining weight, no matter how much food they eat. And birds with roundworms are easily spotted because you can see the worms in their droppings. If you do suspect one or more of your birds is infested with worms, you can purchase inexpensive worm medication at your local farm supply store.

Molting

If you see any of your chickens suddenly losing their feathers, this doesn't necessarily mean anything is wrong with them. They could just be going through a normal molting. Molting is a natural process whereby chickens exchange old feathers for new ones. Older birds usually molt once per year, usually in the summer or fall, although young birds may molt twice in one year. The entire molting process can take anywhere from six to twelve weeks to complete. A molting chicken should not be a cause for alarm and there is nothing special you need to do to treat them. Let the natural process take its course.

EGGS, EGGS, EGGS!

There are so many reasons why people get into backyard chickens. Some raise them as pets. Others raise fancy show birds and enjoy taking their rare breeds to different contests at various state fairs and other events. Still others raise chickens for their fresh meat. And of course, one of the most popular reasons why people raise their own chickens is for a steady supply of fresh eggs. And I suspect that is the reason why you're reading this manual right now. Therefore, let's take a good look at what you need to know about eating the eggs your backyard chickens produce.

Egg Color – Does It Matter?

One of the more interesting things about raising your own chickens is that different breeds of chickens lay different color eggs. Some of them lay those picture-perfect white eggs (like you see in the grocery store) while others lay brown eggs and still others lay eggs of different colors – like blue. You can easily end up with eggs of various colors if you have different breeds of hens. But here's the important thing...don't get hung up on the color of the shell. White eggs aren't any tastier than brown eggs or vice versa. They are all the same on the inside.

Are They Safe To Eat?

If fresh chickens weren't safe to eat, the millions of people who ate them years ago (prior to modern refrigeration, etc.) would have been in a constant state of sickness. But we know that wasn't the case. Draw your own conclusion.

Although countless people enjoy fresh eggs from their own chickens, it is very important to point out that you really should wash them prior to eating them. Even though the edible contents are protected by an outer shell, salmonella is found in the feces of chickens (yes, chicken feces is commonly found on the outside of the eggs). Don't take the chance of accidentally getting any of this into your meal when you crack the egg for its contents. Commercial egg producers wash their eggs thoroughly and so should you.

Another thing to consider before you eat an egg produced by your chickens is how much time has passed between the egg being laid and your eating it. As long as you refrigerate (or eat) the eggs you collect on the same day they are laid, you should be fine. However, if for some reason you go a few days between collecting eggs and you aren't sure how long the eggs have been in the roost, you should definitely discard those eggs.

Can You Eat A Fertilized Egg?

The short answer is yes, you can eat an egg that has been fertilized by a rooster. As long as you refrigerate the egg the same day it was laid, it will not develop into an embryo.

Storing Eggs

Before you store any eggs you should definitely wash them to make sure all bird droppings have been removed. You don't want to take the chance of transferring salmonella to any other foods in your refrigerator.

Although eggs can be safely stored in a cool, dark place, (like they did before modern refrigeration), it really is best to keep them in your refrigerator. Eggs stored in a refrigerator will stay good for up to six weeks.

Did you know you can freeze eggs for later use? It's true. You can keep frozen eggs for up to one year. If you do store eggs this way, it's best to crack them first and store the contents of the egg in some sort of airtight container. You can freeze eggs in their shells but they will probably crack.

DON'T BREAK THIS ONE RULE!

We've covered a lot of ground as we've gone over the different things you should know if you are considering raising chickens in your own backyard. There is, however, one very important rule you should never, ever break in your backyard chicken ventures.

The one rule you should never, ever break is:

Have fun!

Seriously! Raising chickens should always be something you enjoy doing. But really, it's about so much more than gathering your own fresh eggs. It's about knowing where your own food comes from and that it was treated humanely. It's about enjoying the quirky company of these funny little birds. And it's about the incredible feeling of accomplishment you get from raising your flock.

May all of your birds stay healthy and may all of your eggs be tasty.

Printed in the USA
CPSIA information can be obtained
at www.ICGtesting.com
LVHW092154070924
790454LV00008B/408

9 798452 258896